SLEEP SMARTER

Zoe McKey is a bestselling author in the field of self-development. She has lived on her own from a young age, which has shaped her sense of tenacity, perseverance, and self-worth. She brings over ten years of practical knowledge in her books.

SLEEP SMARTER

SLEEPING TIPS TO GET MORE ENERGIZED, PRODUCTIVE AND HEALTHY THE NEXT DAY

ZOE MCKEY

Published by
Rupa Publications India Pvt. Ltd 2021
7/16, Ansari Road, Daryaganj
New Delhi 110002

Sales centres:
Allahabad Bengaluru Chennai
Hyderabad Jaipur Kathmandu
Kolkata Mumbai

Copyright © Zoe McKey 2021

The views and opinions expressed in this book are the author's own and the facts are as reported by her which have been verified to the extent possible, and the publishers are not in any way liable for the same.

All rights reserved.

No part of this publication may be reproduced, transmitted, or stored in a retrieval system, in any form or by any means, electronic, mechanical, photocopying, recording or otherwise, without the prior permission of the publisher.

ISBN: 978-93-90547-37-1

First impression 2021

10 9 8 7 6 5 4 3 2 1

Printed at Nutech Print Services, Faridabad

This book is sold subject to the condition that it shall not, by way of trade or otherwise, be lent, resold, hired out, or otherwise circulated, without the publisher's prior consent, in any form of binding or cover other than that in which it is published.

CONTENTS

Introduction vii

1. Start Your Day with the Evening 1
2. Processing and Planning 6
3. Preparing Physically and Mentally 28
4. Personal Growth in the Right Environment 46
5. Sleeping Habits 57
6. Preparations for a Good Night's Sleep 64
7. Evening Routine for Parents 70
8. What about Those Who Can't Sleep Early? 86
9. Do's and Don'ts 93

Reference 101
Communication and Confidence Coaching 103
Endnotes 107

INTRODUCTION

Since I started my own business, I became obsessed with routines and productivity hacks. Making the big leap from the nine-to-five job to becoming self-employed required many changes. I didn't even think that much about routines before I was self-employed. I had routines, so to say. I had to wake up at seven in the morning to get to work at eight. After work I attended a gym, or some classes at the university. In the evening I had to run to my other job. Sunday was all about chores, sleeping and meeting people. Then repeat.

I didn't have time to even think about routines. When someone casually mentioned to me that I could organize my life better, I should work smarter and that with this life pace I could expect an early death, I just laughed.

"I don't have time for dying, don't worry."

Today, however, I see that I could have handled things much differently. When someone's in a full speed rat race, it's very difficult to see clearly. If I had this book three years, even four years ago, my life could have been so much easier and happier.

I'm sure that there are many people out there who need a book like this just as much as I did. This is why I decided to write it. To help you, busy souls, to maximize and enjoy that little free time between your job and sleeping.

This book is a collection of the how-to's and how-not-to's of famous people, infamous people, and regular people. It is an action book with step-by-step exercises and thorough explanations. I structured the book in a very transparent and easy-to-follow way. The tasks I present are built upon each other, and for a better understanding, I present them through the story of John, a typical office worker who desperately wants a promotion.

As you progress in the book, you'll encounter physical and mental exercises, special tips for parents, and a long summary list of do's and don'ts at the end of the book.

The more I learned about their routines, the more I realized how much I missed out on, how differently could I have done things, and how much easier life could be with the right daily planning. My tips, research and personal experience regarding optimal routine development far exceed a writer's savoir faire.

If I may be so bold to mention, it's much harder to keep your day together if you have your own business. You have unlimited time (I hope a hooded figure with a scythe didn't jerk his head up to this statement), in an unlimited space, no rules, and no workplace demands. You become what you make of your day. If you're not doing anything consistent, or do a thousand things without a focus, it won't carry you very far.

We all have twenty-four hours in a day. Some of us have to deal with one job, two jobs, kids, an education, parents, illness—I could go on. It is nearly impossible to keep all this together without a structure. We all aim for more than simple completion of our goals. We want to do a good job, produce high-quality work. We want to be present when we spend time with our loved ones, and be mindful of ourselves when we need to crack the code of chaos.

Cracking this code is actually easier than it seems. In this book, I'll prove it to you. But before that, let's play. Let's use the power of visualization to get to the land of dreams. So, just relax, and take a few deep breaths.

Imagine yourself waking up in your bed tomorrow morning. Feel that it will be the perfect day. Your body vibrates with energy and impatience to start your day. You feel productive and present. This condition lasts all day. You slay work, you're kind and patient with your kids, and dirty with your spouse. How would you feel at the end of such a day?

What if I told you that it's possible to extend these "perfect" days into perfect weeks and months? To what heights could these days take you in a year or two?

Now, coming back to Earth after such a heavenly visualization, you might think that this sounds awesome, but what's the key? How can you have such an energized morning?

I'm about to tell you.

If you think that your day starts when you open your eyes in the morning, you're not entirely right. The consequence of an energized, carefree morning is a restful night, and the condition of a restful night is a well-executed day that closes with the evening.

Do you know why average restaurants have above-average coffee and desserts? It's the last thing on the menu that you eat. And if the last bites are good, that leaves an overall satisfaction in you as a customer. If the food is excellent but the dessert is awful, you'll leave the restaurant with a bitter taste.

The same applies for your day. If your day had ups and downs but you close it with a good evening routine, you'll feel satisfied, sleep with peace of mind and wake in good spirits. If you had a great day, but waste your evening, by the time you go to sleep, you'll feel less happy about it.

It is very easy to lose track in the evening. After a long day, with your batteries reaching red and saying twenty percent or below, it's highly probable that you won't sit and plan the ideal evening, as you'd do it with a one-hundred-percent full, green battery.

After a long day, evening for most people is just a handful of hours spent in numbness and idleness in front of the computer or TV, eating some fast food and contemplating about the meaninglessness of life.

I work all day, and this is all I can expect afterward? Is this what I'm living for?

This is a tough question. Often our darkest thoughts come to the surface when we are tired and idle. Nevertheless, it is true that for many of us, those few evening hours represent life in the weekdays. This is why it is important to intentionally choose what we do with this short, precious time of day. Routines in the evening can mean peace of mind for the night, and thus, energy for the morning.

Becoming intentional with your evenings is the best thing you can do to aid "tomorrow".

1

START YOUR DAY WITH THE EVENING

"As you make your bed, so you'll sleep and dream."

—Hungarian proverb

John was a murderer. He brutally killed his third alarm clock this year and it was only February. But, he couldn't help it. He felt so exhausted each morning that he did it somewhat instinctively.

He was working on his new project until late—again. However, he couldn't afford the luxury of not doing it. He had high hopes with this project. If he successfully pushed it down the neck of the marketing department of his company, he might get promoted. He must do it, if he wants to improve his life in the long run.

John was a sociable person. He could hang out on social media for hours. He knew he should start working on his project earlier, but he rationalized his need for his social media routine as a disconnection from his job. Although he knew social media was not the most valuable activity to spend each of his evenings with, it was an easy choice.

Around eight or nine at night, after a three-hour disconnection, he ate a heavy dinner. During the day he didn't pay too much attention on what he ate. He just grabbed some snacks. Dinner was his main and only normal meal during the day. After he stuffed himself, he sat on his computer and started working. Food coma was torturing him for a good hour after dinner so his work session was not too productive in the beginning. He resiliently struggled with the project until midnight or later. With his buzzing brain, he couldn't fall asleep till much later but the alarm clock rang mercilessly at six in the morning.

What do you think about John's story? Does it resemble yours? Don't get lost in the details. You don't need to work on a project to stay up late because of mismanaged time. You can play games, read, floss the cat—anything you do instead of sleeping in your precious sleeping hours will twist your next day.

The market is full of books with great morning routines that can help you start your day off on the right foot. However, there aren't nearly as many that talk about the best evening routines that can ensure you an energized and productive morning.

Complementing your morning routines with solid evening routines will help you improve your focus, memory and creativity throughout the day. Evening and morning habits are time and energy-winning mechanisms that make you more productive in general. They can also help you prioritize.

I'd like to refer to the quote from the beginning of this chapter, "*As you make your bed, so you'll sleep and dream.*" Its English equivalent might be, "As you make your bed, so you must lie in it". The quote reflects reality perfectly. If you live a just and righteous life where you have no regrets, you'll have peace of mind. If you have regrets and unfinished businesses, you won't.

It is phrased in a very smart way: it doesn't say that if you have a just life, you'll wake up as a rocket ready to blast. No. It says that you'll rest well. There is a lot of wisdom hidden in these old word-of-mouth sayings. If we take the meaning literally, this proverb is still a good fit: we have better sleep in clean surroundings, a well-made bed rather than on top of our piled clothes and books with our quilt on the ground, right?

Without further ado and persuasion about the importance of evening routines, I'd like to highlight the points that are the main elements of a highly effective evening routine:

- Processing today
- Planning tomorrow
- Nourishing your body and mind
- Dedicating twenty minutes for self-development
- Being cozy in your surroundings
- Disconnecting
- Flexibility

In the following chapters, I will talk about each of these elements of a successful evening routine,and more.

Chapter 2 will present the processing and planning phase, which are the motors of a successful evening routine.

In Chapter 3, I will tell you the best ways to nourish your body and mind. The tips and advice are from professionals and high performers. My opinion is merely an extension of them.

Chapter 4 will unfold what I mean by twenty minutes for self-development, how to create the "right" surroundings for yourself and why it's important to disconnect.

Chapter 5 will be a crutch for parents—especially those ones who have younger children. I had been talking with full-time moms, full-time working moms, engaged and less engaged dads and based on theirs and specialists' advice, I put together a special evening routine schedule for parents.

I designed Chapter 6 to be a short, concise summary of everything you read in this book divided into Do and Don't categories. There is also a surprise hidden in Chapter 6, but I won't spoil it for now.

By the time you finish reading this short, informative book, you'll know how to manage your evening, and therefore your morning, your day and your entire life better.

2

PROCESSING AND PLANNING

"Give me six hours to chop down a tree and I will spend the first four sharpening the axe."

—Abraham Lincoln

Do you remember John? He is the guy with a job and a separate project he works on for a promotion. And has crazy-long social media chatters. He just bought his fourth alarm clock of the year today. If you ever wondered why he doesn't use his smart phone instead of an actual alarm clock, I'd just like to briefly hint the price difference between three-dollar simplicity and a six-hundred-dollar phone. He's a practical guy.

John has realized that something is wrong with his life. Recently, he is exhausted and negative, even though he used to be a jolly fellow who always had time for some mischief and actual, face-to-face meetings. He decided to make a change in his life. Whatever the reason was for his fatigue and foul mood has to be stopped. To act upon his decision, he collected every piece of information, every single thing he did when he felt he had the time and was genuinely cheerful. Then he compared those actions to what he does now. What changed?

What's the only thing John forgot about among his work commitments? Nothing less than himself. He has totally ignored his needs as a human being and gave everything he had to others—his time, his energy, and his wellbeing. He has to change as quickly as possible because he is at the limits of his stress bearing and energy. He collected everything he wanted to change about his free time. His free time consisted of those few hours in the evening after arriving home.

The Right Goals

Now you think I'm about to say, "John decided to quit his job and become a free spirit" etc. No, not at all. He liked his job. He didn't want to quit, he didn't want more free time, or less challenges. He just wanted the time he had to be spent better. And to be more energized during the day he had to spend at his job. Not all of us want to be entrepreneurs, artists and wayfarers. Most of the people aren't and don't really want to become one. Otherwise they'd already be. Am I negative here? No, I'm not.

Do you want to have twenty-four hours to play with? Do you want the unpredictable life schedule and income of an entrepreneur? Do you want to wander in the wild and live in cheap hostels? Or to sell your own work online?

If you'd say, "Yes, I do," I'd raise my brow in a Don Corleone kind of way and say, "I don't believe you." So you'd become offended and insist that becoming an entrepreneur, let's say, is very important to you. It's your long cherished dream. You could repeat it to me as many times as you wanted and I still wouldn't believe. You know why?

Because they are just words. They don't represent your true, heart-felt values. Only your actions do. How can I be sure about this?

I wanted to become a professional fitness model since I left puberty. I go to the gym regularly, I talk about it endlessly. Each year will be *the* year, for more than twelve years now. One of my smart friends once asked me, "Aren't you tired of fooling yourself with this goal of yours?" I was shocked. "I beg your pardon?" I asked disapprovingly, starting to enumerate the reasons why I couldn't do it until now. I had one every year.

"You've been talking about this goal since 2006. If you really wanted it, you've done it by now. I think you like the idea of being a fitness model but you don't like anything that comes with being a fitness model—the hard trainings, the Spartan diet, the financial and time investment. And you like fries and ice-cream way too much. You say that you'd be able to do all these sacrifices but your actions tell it otherwise."

Wow. My friend nailed it so deeply and correctly that I couldn't even argue. Do you live in a similar self-deception regarding your goals? If you do, I have two suggestions. One, stop it and redefine your goals based on your past actions. Two, stop making excuses and find a way to do what you want.

Why did I tell this story? To help you choose your evening routines for the right reasons. Whatever time you spend on talk but not taking action becomes wasted. The more you talk, the more time, creative energy, motivation, and hope you waste.

If you're like me, and you plan to do something amazing but you know you'll never be able to pay its price, forget about it. You're wasting energy and potential by daydreaming instead of focusing on what would really make a change in your life. If you hate unpredictability, the lack of an authority figure (boss) who makes sure you'll get your job done, you're not disciplined and so on, entrepreneurship would be a struggle for you. And you probably know that. Entrepreneurship sounds appealing but you could never sacrifice safety for risk. This is why you never started your own business.

If I'm wrong, I apologize. You have another option in this case: start acting instead of talking. Security and timing can be a good excuse for a short while. You don't want to be reckless and that's good. But just like in dating, if the potential partner delays the date a second and third time, he's just not that into you. The same applies to your "dream," you're just not that into it.

Please, please, turn your thoughts towards the right reasons before you start implementing a new routine. Otherwise your new routines won't stick. If you're preparing to change your lifestyle compared to the current one, the routines you adopt matching today's needs will become outdated before they'd truly stick. Also, they may not match your changed needs. If you're sure you'll change your life for good, adjust your new routines to empower the new lifestyle. For example, if you already handed in your notice and you're about to leave town to join a fire dancing group in a circus, don't start adopting routines which are tailored to your current nine-to-five lifestyle. You'll be done with that within a month. Better arm yourself up with evening routines that aid the hectic life of a circus performer.

If you adopt the new routines adjusting them to the "life you hope to live for ten years but you know it will never happen," your efforts will be in vain again. In this case, the routines won't fit your current life. For example, if you want to become a nurse instead of an accountant for ten years but you're still pulling papers instead of diapers, maybe you shouldn't adopt evening routines that match the twelve–twenty-four work schedule of a nurse. Extreme examples, but you get the gist.

I assume you're reading this book because you are willing to put an effort in developing at least one new, good routine in your life. The most important attributive of a routine is its length. Routines are long-term plans. You're willing to invest the money (this book), and the time into them. Make these two efforts worth by choosing the best routines that aid your true needs.

Process the Day

Processing the day means running through the main events of the day in the evening. What were the most important obligations you had to fulfill? What were the happy moments and what were the least pleasant, yet educational ones? This is a step that you can execute on your way home from work, during grocery shopping, or while creating a relaxing atmosphere after you arrive home. Timing is up to you. This task only requires mental presence.

If you feel that you cannot highlight any important accomplishment that day, that's a problem. It means that your energy was divided between many insignificant or minor tasks, instead of grouping your time, attention and focus on specific, important objectives. It makes a huge difference in the evening if you feel that your day was meaningful, and you actually accomplished something, or it just went by like a handful of pointless hours.

Exercise

If you think you can't highlight any meaningful accomplishments in your days, consider changing it. If you don't do anything about it, you risk living your life with a conscious, or subconscious, a feeling of meaninglessness. Think back to a tiring day when you did a great job, and achieved something you previously proposed yourself. Even if you felt tired physically, your mind was buzzing.

Now recall a lazy day at your office when there was

nothing to do, and thus you did nothing. Even if the day wasn't tiring, at the end of it you felt exhausted and mentally as active as a pair of socks.

Why do people choose comfort even though they know that getting stuff done makes them feel much better about themselves? Because comfort is pain-free. People fear pain and discomfort. In the moments of fear it seems more reasonable to avoid unpleasant events than to take risk, achieve something, solve a problem, and be satisfied afterwards. Why?

Because today you are conditioned to think that pain and discomfort are abnormal events in life. Today the ground zero is unlimited happiness, and everybody who is below this standard does something wrong. You don't use the law of attraction well enough, you don't love yourself strong enough, you're not rich enough and so on. We live in the age of more, bigger, better. Opportunities seem unlimited. Commercials bamboozle you with their awesome products that will turn you into Mr. Bombastic. However, when you buy the product, you still feel the same sad loser you were before, with an expensive watch and an empty pocket. You hate feeling a sad loser, so now you turn your attention towards something different that can solve this issue for you. Another gadget, a book, a seminar, some drugs, food, a cat… But regardless of how much you want to repress your pain, it will still be there. Anytime the effect of a new purchase wears off (and it often wears off quicker than your money reproduction) you'll fall back to your sad reality.

What do you do when you're sadden by your reality? You turn to others' realities. What is the best place to choke on others' realities? The "my-life-is-the-best-social-media," of course. But people always seems happy, skinny, eating tasty things, and doing fun stuff while you sit at home, being sad, polishing your watch. It is almost unavoidable not to think that something must be wrong with you. If every other person is happy and only you are not, then something is off about you.

Feeling so uniquely sad will drop your motivation below zero. You'll go through your days feeling how worthless they are, thinking it's not even worth hoping for something better because it will never come. It is a self-enforcing process: the less value and challenge you find in your life, the more demotivated you'll become. The more demotivated you are, the less power you'll feel to do anything. Oh, did I mention that solving problems, setting tasks for the day is scary? Add the painful, motivation-free state you're in to the fright and you'll get the best recipe for how to feel meaningless.

What happens next? People get comfortable, start

taking things for granted, and strive to live their lives without any pain, discomfort, or problems. You, me, that dude sitting next to you listening to Beats music terribly loudly—we're all trapped in the comfort of the 21st century. We hate pain, we hate the uncomfortable feeling of insecurity, we hate slow Internet, we hate to stand on the bus, and we hate our problems, because, oh boy, we have a lot of them. What to buy for dinner, which cell phone package to choose, how to get back the ten dollars we lost, or how to avoid the nosy neighbor—tragedies. Recently, I've caught myself whining about such ridiculous "problems" that my virtual past self-slaps me, saying, "Shut up. You're miserable because you choose to be."

That's right. I'm miserable because I let myself be miserable. I certainly have much easier problems to solve now than I did five years ago. I should be happy for that.

Problems are not the problem. Rich, poor, fat, slim, smart, simple—everybody has problems. Just some people have better problems.

Problems, as phenomena, are constant in one's life. They are necessary. What's more, problems are the door to a good life. Solving problems creates happiness, as well as more problems, which leads to more opportunities to achieve happiness.

For example, if you order home delivery to solve your no-time-for-cooking problem, you'll be relieved and happy. But on the other hand, you'll create other problems. Somebody has to be home to receive the food package. Often, home delivery is more expensive than if you'd bought the ingredients at a grocery store. Now you have to find an optimal solution to these problems. Or if you finally can find three hours in your Sundays to visit your parents, and you solve the problem of a lack of contact, you'll have to put up with new issues such as finding the optimal traffic time zone or route, what to bring to your parents, what to talk about, etc.

You won't get rid of problems. But you can create new, better ones by solving the old, bitter ones. The emphasis is on solving, moving forward, not getting stuck in self-pity or avoidance. It's not your problems that make you feel miserable, but your avoidance of them. The very thing you do to feel better about your problems is what makes you feel bad. It's not your problems that make you unhappy, but fear, sloth, or ignorance in addressing them.

Human beings like to feel useful, canny, and smart. They need to fix and solve stuff. It makes them feel accomplished, satisfied...*happy*. When someone is avoiding solving a problem, they are fostering themselves from these positive feelings. I make problem-solving sound easy. It is not as easy as I make it sound, but it is not too complicated either. People are just mostly lazy and fearful to address some problems because it requires a certain amount of discomfort. As I said earlier, discomfort is not the friend of the smoothie generation.

If happiness comes from solving problems, it means that it is the result of an activity, not of idleness or magic incantations. Happiness doesn't reside in stationary elements like having a certain amount of money, possessing two or three degrees, or having Henry Cavill as your husband. Stuff like that won't make you happy on their own. Helping someone or solving a problem with your money, inventing something uniquely helpful thanks to your knowledge, or being able to find a common solution to your anxieties with your husband brings you happiness.

Happiness is not the goal; it's a work-in-progress. Our entire lives are a work in progress. Don't work to get rid of problems—work to have problems you enjoy fixing. It isn't the worst thing to solve the problem of finding the best Italian restaurant in town, is it? Or selecting the dance style that best fits your personality? There are less "first-world" problems out there, for sure.

Challenges keep us in motion and alive. Without targets, days can turn into a pointless mass of hours.

Therefore, the best you can do for yourself in the evenings is to set some goals for the next day. I like the magic of number three, so let's say, set three tasks for yourself for the next day. These tasks can be about anything, solving a minor problem like paying a bill, or a bigger one, like having *that* conversation with your husband.

Emphasized tasks are like a magnifying glass in the sun. If you concentrate the light on a tiny point, that thing will catch fire. The same goes for your energy and attention: if you focus on a specific task your work and life will start to make sparks, and even catch fire, in the best sense of the saying. Live intentionally. Solve your problems. Feel proud and grateful. Do one thing for yourself every day, a painful or uncomfortable one. Get out of your daze of self-pity. Believe it or not, all those happy people around you struggle with some issues. Their problems might not be the same as yours but they certainly have some. Even if their problems are better than yours, it doesn't mean that they don't feel equally frustrated.

The goal is to solve these problems. The key is to have something done at the end of the day that surpassed your comfort level.

When you process your day in the evening, recall the problem or task you were working on and ask the following questions:

What did I do regarding the task that went well?
What did I do regarding the task that didn't go well?
What did I not do regarding the task, making it not go well?
What did I not do regarding the task that made it go well?
How can I improve?

Addressing these questions gives you a thorough self-evaluation, and helps you see where you did do well and what needs improvement.

Did You Know?

Benjamin Franklin, the famed Colonial American innovator and patriot, discovered the importance of evening routines quite early. Each day before going to bed, he asked himself: "What good have I done today?"

Then he took a few minutes to answer this question. He had other rituals before sleeping that he summarized like this: "Put things in their places, supper, music or diversion or conversation, and examination of the day." He was quite consistent about his rituals.

Try his method. Compress your day into five minutes. This meditative practice will help you to switch from work mode to "you" mode. Processing your day in those five minutes will often help you to remember tasks that you did not accomplish—maybe because they slipped your mind, or because they simply didn't fit in the day.

Collect these tasks and write them down on a reminder pad if they still have relevance. Keeping a record of unfinished tasks and scheduling them for the next day will give you peace of mind. You will know that you won't forget them now. Put the list in a visible place to remember them for when you can take action to finish them. Then, move on to something else. Know that you don't need to worry, they are listed, and won't be forgotten again.

It doesn't matter what processing method you pick, as long as your day is fully reviewed. Be consistent about your daily objectives. Don't propose more to yourself than you know you can accomplish. Don't set the target to write an entire book the next day because you won't be able to meet your own goal. This will leave you with a sense of failure. Be rational with your tasks. You can't fix your entire marriage with one conversation, you won't improve your work ethic by being hyperactive for one day, you won't become friends with someone after one meeting… Be real. Sometimes people have goals and are open to solve problems, they just bit a bigger amount than they could chew in a day. They will feel the same outcome when they process their day as those who didn't do anything. Keep your plans real and you won't have sleepless nights, tossing and turning with the cloudy torment of a possible unfinished business.

Planning Tomorrow

Do this step after the processing phase. When you do the processing phase, all your thoughts are focused on the near past day and the present moment. Planning, however, is about focusing on the near future. Plan the tasks that bear a special importance for tomorrow.

Exercise

Plan your next day. "Paper is to write things down that we need to remember. Our brains are used to think," as Albert Einstein smartly phrased it. Write down everything you can think of that you need to do tomorrow. This shouldn't take more than five to ten minutes. Do you feel reluctant to put something on paper because that task seems an exquisite pain in the proverbial back? Write that one down first. Overcoming your procrastination and sense of discomfort regarding a task will give you triple fulfillment at the end of the day.

When you finished collecting your tasks-to-be-done for tomorrow, rank them based on importance. Which ones have top priority? Which are not so urgent? The top items are the tasks you want to spend your time on. Let's call them TPTs—top priority tasks. Remember, if you set too many tasks for yourself but you fail achieving them, you'll feel dissatisfied. Keep the amount and difficulty of your tasks real. Too easy tasks will backfire at the end of the day just like the too difficult ones. If your only objective is to take the trash out, you won't feel very good about your accomplishments in the evening.

The TPTs are your highest value objectives. These tasks will make the largest to your life. TPTs are often jobs that you and only you can execute, problems no one else can solve, etc. It is important to have balance with the personal and work related TPTs. For example, if you focus only on work-related tasks, your relationship will suffer sooner or later. If you get too dwelled in your relationship, your career will be neglected. Keep balance, one or two things to do, solve or improve in your personal life and one or two in your professional.

Keep a strategic reminder about the threats to the successful completion of your TPTs. For example, getting distracted on social media. If you're conscious about the roadblocks that can sabotage your success, you can prepare yourself to avoid them.

Having troubles with avoiding social media presence? Download the app, Self-Control. This app was life changing to me. I'm using it right now. The point of the program is that you can exclude yourself from different websites for certain amount of time. You can choose to block yourself out of however many sites you want from ten minutes to twenty-four hours. The trick is: there is no antidote. If you're out, you're out for good. You can't rewrite your order in the program. You have to wait the given time to run out before accessing the blocked sites again. This is why I never lock myself out for more than four hours. My productivity cycle won't last more than that time in one sitting anyway. I block myself out of social media sites, shopping sites, for four hours. When the time is off, I check everything as a resting period, and then I restart the four hours block again.

You cannot control everything that happens around you, but at least you can take control of the things you can influence. A little distraction here, another coffee there, and like magic an hour has disappeared. Be strong and resist temptations. Otherwise, you'll feel sorry for the time wasted and you risk not finishing your TPTs.

If you're not able to finish a task knowing you could have done things differently, it will leave a bitter taste in your mouth. This kind of stress generation is harmful and totally avoidable.

Do you have difficulty saying no when someone's interrupting you? I know you try to be nice when you say yes to any little stupid nonsense others bother you with but look at it this way: whenever you're nice with someone when you'd have other personal priorities, you're not nice with yourself.

No means no. You don't have to be rude about it. If you're in the middle of something and interrupting would be a headache, just tell people kindly, but firmly, that you can't help them right now. Set a time when you will be able to take care of their problems. However, for now, your task prevails.

Another enemy of the successful completion of TPTs is the deadly urge to procrastinate. The habit of delaying slows down all development. It crashes your goals and replaces action with despair.

Track the side activities you often do and the amount of time you spend on each of them. Knowing the precise duration of your side activities will give you an accurate picture of how much time you "waste" on them and how much should you reduce to be able to finish your tasks without worrying.

Clutter creates distractions, discomfort, hampers

efficiency, and decreases performance. Throw away (or give away) everything that is unnecessary. Then, organize the rest of your things. Let your workplace be transparent and tidy.

Distractions can sabotage your plans. Find yours and deactivate them.

> *"Know the enemy and know yourself; in a hundred battles you will never be in peril. When you are ignorant of the enemy, but know yourself, your chances of winning or losing are equal. If ignorant both of your enemy and yourself, you are certain in every battle to be in peril."*
>
> —Sun Tzu

Now, you may think that identifying all your roadblocks and figuring a method to disarm them would take an enormous amount of time in your evenings. Not at all. Thinking about your main traps is rather a one-time time investment than a repetitive one. You identify the roadblock and its antidote and then you use the same antidote every time the roadblock shows up. The list needs to be expanded only if you observe a new distraction invading your mind.

Writing a few tasks for the next day and prioritizing

them shouldn't take more than ten minutes, either. Fifteen minutes tops, but then you must have a time-consuming debate about which tasks are to be the TPTs.

If you feel that you should do more than three or four TPTs a day, relax. There are always more tasks than time. There are too many good books to read, people to meet, projects to improve, and missions to accomplish to get your life's objectives to zero. I will tell you a secret: you will never get caught up with everything you want to do. The more you realize and accept this, the closer will you get to a less stressful life with fewer tasks accomplished daily.

You have two options in handling life. You can choose to run around like a basket-case trying to catch up on everything and accomplishing nothing. Or you can plan, prioritize and execute your top priority tasks and problems.

John decided to break his regular after-work habit. When he finished his job, he decided to walk home instead of squeezing himself onto a bus. He used this time to process his day. It was a good thirty-minute walk, so he had plenty of time to think things through, and evaluate his accomplishments. By the time he got home he didn't feel the need to go on social media to relax. He already felt relaxed.

He made some notes about the observations he

made after the processing session. He wrote down some new thoughts on how can he save even more time. By processing his day, he identified some time gaps where he did totally useless things, like queuing almost twenty minutes at lunchtime. He figured that he can go earlier or later to eat, thus he can save the time spent in queuing and do something more productive instead.

After this brilliant idea, he took a warm shower with a satisfied grin. During his shower he brainstormed about the next day's tasks. He carefully planned what he wanted to focus on the next day.

3

PREPARING PHYSICALLY AND MENTALLY

"Mens sana in corpore sano."

—Latin Proverb

John almost killed the alarm. But, this time he was not that tired since he went to bed relatively early. He decided to stop working on his project at 11 p.m. The biggest change compared to the morning before was that he finally had a purpose to wake up to. He had three problems that he needed to solve. He felt motivated to wake up, wanted to set his plans into action and prove himself that he is able to succeed.

Physical and Mental Nourishment

Decrease decision fatigue

The human body is not an inexhaustible source of energy. It needs rest, food, and water to generate power. If these power supplies are reduced or denied, the body will struggle to think, to do well, to be happy and survive in general. If someone lets his body to be so run down, no wonder that his productivity, creativity, patience and joyfulness level decreases drastically.

Most people have their mental and physical energy levels at their peak in the first few hours after waking up, following a good seven to eight hours sleep. People have different circadian rhythms. The National Institute of General Medical Sciences defines circadian rhythms as: "physical, mental, and behavioral changes that follow a roughly twenty-four-hour cycle, responding primarily to light and darkness in an organism's environment." They also influence bodily functions like hormone releases and body temperature regulation.

Each choice you make during the day uses up a certain amount of your energy. And you have to make many decisions in a day. The phenomena of getting tired by the amount of decisions you make is called *decision fatigue*.

The more you reduce the amount of trivial decisions in your lives, the better.

Steve Jobs, for example, wore the same black turtleneck, Levi's jeans and sports shoes precisely for the reason to avoid the tiring and time-consuming decision of what he should wear. He never had to put up with problems like "I've got nothing to wear! I don't have a piece of rag to put on," as we ladies sometimes do.

As your energy level decreases during the day, each decision becomes harder and harder to make. At one point your tired brain will start to look for shortcuts. These shortcuts either manifest as impulsive actions, or as the avoidance of making the decision itself.

If you act impulsively you may say or do things you don't mean and cause a lot of headache for yourself later. If you keep avoiding important decisions, you can easily end up being labeled as irresponsible, or a notorious avoider. If the decisions you don't make are related to your health and wellbeing, they can backfire bitterly in the long run.

Being exhausted mentally is more dangerous than being exhausted physically, because you are not consciously aware of being tired. The emptier your mental energy tank gets as the end of the day approaches, the easier it is to break promises and procrastinate on resolutions. After several hours of active decision-making, your willpower tank gets empty regardless of the nature of the decisions. Spend your energy on the important decisions first.

You may think now, *okay, I get it, too many decisions suck the energy out of me, but what should I do to avoid decision fatigue?*

The answer is simple: make fewer decisions. The fewer decisions you have to make, the less tired you'll be at the end of the day—both physically and mentally. Therefore, you'll have more energy and capacity to do things for yourself in your free time.

Exercise

This exercise challenges you to figure out three ways you can reduce decision fatigue in your life. Write down three decisions you can skip to make from tomorrow on.

I will give you some examples, but do not take these as your solution unless they would indeed fit in your life and would make it easier.

One example of decision fatigue reduction can be my previous example with the late Steve Jobs and his pre-decided way of dressing. The time and energy he saved with simplifying his choice of outfit invested into developing his life's work, the Apple products. He did a pretty good job there.

Another decision preservation technique can be what

CEOs of large companies do. They have lots of assistants around them. Secretaries, gatekeepers, virtual assistants shield them from the thousands of questions they would otherwise face. Delegating these distractions to others, company leaders can focus on running and growing their organizations.

If you are not a CEO you don't need a gatekeeper and a secretary. You can still delegate your tasks to others. Take the delegation process to more humble grounds. For example, divide certain house or child-related tasks with your partner. Agree that you take care of you part of decision-making but you don't want to deal with your spouse's part. Trust each other's judgment and liberate yourself from decision fatigue.

You can save time and energy on decisions by making them the night before. That's right. You can always use your time in the evening to decide some not-top priority tasks (NTPTs) in advance.

These NTPTs can be:

Prepare your breakfast in advance. Maybe your lunch for work, too.

Prepare what you will wear the next day. Be thorough about it, think about all the clothes you'll need during your next day: working clothes, training stuff, umbrella in case of rain and so on.

Pack your working bag in the evening so you wouldn't forget anything in the morning rush.

Here's an extra tip about planning NTPTs: When I had two jobs, my only free day was Sunday. This was the day to do everything—washing, cleaning, cooking, grocery shopping… I got used to thinking in advance on Sundays unless I wanted to torture myself on my busy weekdays.

Each Sunday I planned my week in advance. I had a diary for my planning purposes. Each page was divided into three columns: clothes, food and other. Each page stood for a day from Monday to Saturday. I didn't rest until I filled all the days with all the information I needed. I checked the weather and I planned my daily outfits accordingly.

I set up a six-day meal plan, and did my grocery shopping a week in advance. I knew which days were less and more stressful, which were the ones when I had CrossFit classes. I took hectic days and training days into consideration when choosing my meals. Of course those days were more carbie- and sugar-packed. For Friday and Saturday, I planned menus as advanced as scrambled eggs and rice pudding. I tried to calculate my general level of fatigue and demotivation as the weekend approached. I knew I wouldn't struggle with cooking a full blown Italian dinner on Friday.

Now I made it. If you thought I will help you think simpler, all your hopes flew away reading all my details of thinking in advance. First time it might take you some time, but I guarantee that with practice, considering fatigue level, weather, extra activities and daily stress expectations will come automatically. You might have an intense half an hour thinking session on Sunday but you won't have to think about your meals, clothes and schedules for a week. It's a good trade. You should be well-rested when you do your weekly plan, that's why I insist doing it on your free day.

Don't feel stressed about your weekly plans. If you don't feel like eating burgers on Wednesday, just switch meals between the days. The same applies to clothes. The point is to have a guideline.

Take a little walk after dinner. Try to have an early dinner, then go to a one- or two- mile walk. Make no excuses. It's good to not get too drowsy after dinner, and win a couple of relatively active hours for your evening.

Walking in the evening has sleep aiding benefits. This theory has been proven by the national Sleep Foundation's 2013 "Sleep in America" Poll. Above the sports factor and sleeping aid, walking can increase creativity. When you're walking, your mind isn't working as quickly. This helps you to open the gate for the free flow of ideas. If there is a problem you haven't been able to figure out, a nighttime walk can guide you to a creative solution.

Walking has been the evening practice of Joel Gascoigne, CEO of Buffer. He goes for a twenty-minute walk each night. He claims this helps him to switch off before sleeping. In an interview Gascoigne stated, "This is a wind-down period, and allows me to evaluate the day's work, think about the greater challenges, gradually stop thinking about work, and reach a state of tiredness."

Why Early Dinner?

We all heard about the beneficial factors of going to sleep early. However, recent studies done by scientists proved that keeping "the earlier, the better habit" when it comes to dinner is beneficial. Apart from saving some money on the happy hour meal, there are other reasons why an early dinner is worth considering.

Dr Louis J. Aronne, Director of the Weight Control Program at Weill Cornell Medical College—New York Presbyterian Hospital has studied people's eating habits for a long time, and observed some common patterns. One of his observations was about people who eat late at night. These people tended to eat more than those who chose to consume their last meal earlier.

Studies have also proven that late-night binging can be partially responsible for high triglyceride levels. Triglyceride is a type of fat found in our blood. This fat is generated by unused calories that our body converts. If our blood has high levels of triglycerides, the risk of getting a heart attack or stroke significantly increases.

Early dinner has the promise of better sleep. The National Institute of Health stated that late-night meals can evoke indigestion, which disturbs our sleep. Drinking more than two alcoholic drinks at night can cause the same symptoms—restless, shallow sleep, and more frequent, sudden wake ups. Researchers at the University of Michigan also claim that alcohol or food-related sleeping disorders are worse for women.

Last but not least, having an early dinner can keep you in shape. It even helps losing weight. An experiment with mice in cell metabolism showed that mice that ate within an eight-hour interval and then skipped eating for sixteen hours were slimmer than those mice given the same amount of calories, but in a larger interval of hours. This theory assumes that a longer pause between meals gives the body time to digest the food better.

Scientists notice another interesting phenomenon.

Those mice that ate a high-fat diet, but fasted for sixteen hours gained less weight than those who got the same type of food and calorie amount, but ate more often with less fasting.

David Zinczenko, the author of the best-selling book, *Eat This, Not That*, calls this type of diet the Eight Hour Diet, and actually is a popular weight loss plan. He promises that people will lose serious amounts of pounds, won't be restricted to certain (mostly impossible to follow) meals, but can eat almost everything they want, as long as all their meals can fit in the eight-hour interval and then fast for sixteen hours.

I can recommend you to choose a healthy salad bar or any other protein-full, low-carb food-serving restaurant from where you pick up some packed dinner. Thus you can save the time and energy you'd spend with preparing dinner. Make a treaty with yourself: on weekdays buy some takeaway food so you save some time, but in exchange on the weekends, you cook.

After dinner, go for a short ten- or twenty-minute walk. Try to avoid all kinds of electronic distractions—no music, no podcast. For these few minutes stay inside your mind and observe your thoughts. You can also do the processing or planning if you haven't done it yet. It's a good time to do the daily processing.

A Place for Everything and Everything in Its Place

Oh, boy. I think this was the first sentence my grandma learned when she was a child. Even when she became sick and could hardly move, she still put everything back in its place before going to sleep. She said she couldn't rest until all was in order around her. As a kid, I didn't understand her, but now I can see that she had a point.

On one hand, early evenings are a perfect time to put away those things we used during the day, but would probably hinder us in the morning. By things I mean clothes, dishes, toys, and other appliances. This practice is also good for doing the processing routine for the day. Let me give you a quick reminder of some questions you can ponder while cleaning up: *What were the successes of the day? What didn't go so well? What am I grateful for? Was there anything unexpected? How can I improve?*

If you do a quick tidying each evening and don't let things to pile up, this routine shouldn't last more than five to ten minutes. You'll be very grateful that the clutter won't greet you the next morning. Mornings should be about starting a new day productively, not trying to turn a blind eye on yesterday's unfinished business.

Time to Relax

After a long day, even if you got rid of some minor decision and saved some energy, you'll still feel exhausted. Sitting in front of the computer, standing on your feet and running around, or even sitting in the car for hours, all can turn you into Garfield the lazy cat. Fatigue creates some tension in your brain and your muscles. Don't bring this tension to your bed and sleep with it. Get rid of it first.

A very easy and practical way to release tension is to take a quick, hot shower. Lavender has a calming, relaxing effect. Putting a few drops of lavender oil in the shower, or in an evaporator can do magic.

There are some excellent relaxation massage oils that can do wonders if you rub your tired limbs with them. The best essential oils you can treat yourself to are lavender, ylang ylang and tangerine. To read more about essential oils, check out this site[*].

Gwyneth Paltrow's relaxation routine consists of a well-planned bathing ritual. She considers it the best way to regain calmness at the end of a busy day. In an interview to *Elle* Magazine she said, "I take an Epsom

---

[*]http://www.experience-essential-oils.com/relaxation-massage-oil.html

salt bath every night to wind down. I use a lot of organic essential oils on my pressure points."

Another more active way of relaxation can be stretching. You can combine this exercise with some relaxation music. If you are flexible, or just genuinely interested, you could try a short and relaxing yoga session. However, I must emphasize that you try it on your own responsibility if you have never done yoga before. Even if video tutorials are explicit and thorough, they can't replace an actual teacher. I'd recommend taking a few yoga classes before jumping into home yoga. An instructor can show you exactly how you should execute the exercises, where your limits are, and the maximum effort you should do for improvement.

Stretching, combined with relaxing in the evening, releases your mind and body from tension. There are specific asanas, or yoga positions, that are "designed for an evening practice to wind down the body, helping you move intuitively to stretch away tension and transition from your active day to a relaxed state that is conducive to a good night's sleep."

I follow the recommendation of the yoga and lifestyle site, Verywell Fit, to do ten asanas[*] every other evening.

---

[*]https://www.verywellfit.com/yoga-poses-for-evening-downward-facing-dog-3567172

It is a comprehensive site to get useful information about yoga, watch tutorials, read exercise plans like the one I just linked, and yoga equipment.

In my personal evening routine I have a ten-minute back stretching exercise. Since I work in front of the computer a lot, I started to slouch. After a while my friends told me that I was transforming from Esmeralda into Quasimodo, and I should do something about it.

I went to a physician to ask for advice. She recommended that I use yoga tiles that have become invaluable assets ever since. Each evening before going to bed, I lay the two bricks in a straight line on their thinner side, and I lay with my spine on them. When I'm on the top of the bricks, the first brick supports my head and neck, and the second supports and pulls up my upper body. I keep the rest of my body—lower back, legs, and arms relaxed. I keep the position for ten minutes.

It is painful to execute this back stretching in the beginning, but it is very efficient. If you work in an office, or if you have a hunched back or feel back pain, I can highly recommend this evening routine to improve your posture. Make sure to consult with a physician first. It worked for me, thus I recommend it, but it might not be the best solution for you. Just know that there is a cheap and good solution for Quasimodo syndrome out there.

After you're done with all your evening routines that require you to move, go to bed and lay down. Unless you are so tired that you instantly fall asleep, stay awake for a few more minutes. Keep some books on your nightstand. Have multiple genres so you can pick the one that fits your mood the best that day. Have enlightening, positive, and inspiring books. Choose books that calm you and remind you of what's truly important in life. Let all the peace and delightful vibes coming from the book run through you.

I avoid fiction novels because if a good story captures and intrigues me too much, I won't be able to put the book down. For some people a good fiction story can actually speed up the sleeping process. Some people read just a few pages and then put the book down to imagine what they just read. Their eyes start feeling heavy and they get into dreamland before they realize it.

If you're still awake after reading, regardless of what happened that day, say thank you. Be grateful that you got to live through this day. You had chances to live a happy day, and you'll have chances tomorrow as well. Be grateful that you have a bed to sleep in, and for tomorrow being a new beginning, and for being self-aware enough to realize these things.

Take a few deep breaths. Relax both your mind and

your body. Focusing on your breathing is an easy way to get more relaxed. It's nice to have gratitude and well-oxygenated lungs before falling asleep.

I have one last tip for the evening, which is quite controversial. Some scientists approve it, some advise against it. In my experience, it is a helpful thing to do. Try it, and if you feel uncomfortable, don't do it. Are you curious what I'm talking about? Nothing too fancy, I'm sorry. Here is my ultimate evening health routine tip: drink a tall glass of water in the evening, one and a half hours before you go to sleep. You are about to sleep seven or eight hours, and you won't be drinking any fluids in that time. Water hydrates you, helps your metabolism, cleans your body of toxins, and even helps you eat less. Your body contains at least seventy percent water, and you need to consume water in order to stay healthy.

Alternatively, you can choose to drink warm water. Warm water won't shock your system as much as cold will, so you won't get into an alert wake up state when your body reacts.

Keep a bottle or glass of water next to your bed. Sometimes people wake up during the night because they feel thirsty, but they don't want to go to the kitchen to get a glass. If you wake up because of thirst, it means that your body is in a serious need for water. You need to hydrate yourself. Ease this need by having extra water at hand.

Water fires up your metabolism and speeds up the rate at which new blood cells are produced. The more red blood cells you have, the more oxygen they carry to your brain. If your brain gets more oxygen, you'll become much more alert with a greater ability to focus. Water also helps you get rid of toxins from your body. It balances your lymph glands that help you fight and easily overcome infections. Last but not least, drinking water on an empty stomach cleanses your colon, making it easier to absorb nutrients.

There are some exceptions when it is not advised to drink a large amount of fluids before sleeping. If you suffer from kidney or heart problems, or if you can't fall back to sleep when you get up to use the restroom in the middle of the night, you may want to consider drinking water a few hours before sleeping, and just in the morning when you wake up. Read more about possible risks and benefits on DoctorsHealthPress[*].

John walked home, and he felt very satisfied. He felt he was on a mission. *Now comes the evening!* He was excited and still energetic. He finally had a productive

---

[*]https://www.doctorshealthpress.com/food-and-nutrition-articles/the-benefits-of-drinking-water-before-bedtime/

day. He realized that there were not so many things that should be done in a day, but only some major ones that make a real difference.

On his way home, he dropped into a Japanese restaurant to pick up some salad and sashimi. He ordered the meal on his coffee break in the early afternoon, so he just had to grab it. He saved some minutes there, too. He ate his dinner first thing after getting home. When he took out the garbage, he went for a short walk. The sun was just setting on the horizon, so he took the opportunity to take some inspiring pictures.

After the walk, he got home, took a warm bath, listened to a Nepalese musician's throat singing, which was relaxing and brain-firing at the same time. After the bath, he spent some hours with his project, did a bit of stretching, made his to-do list for the next day, and went to bed so high-spirited he could hardly believe it.

4

PERSONAL GROWTH IN THE RIGHT ENVIRONMENT

"Your outer world is a reflection of your inner world."

—Hal Elrond

All changes come from within. A depressing environment can bring down even the most high-spirited person. Spending time in a place you dislike or even hate, is demotivating. The idea of a routine makeover covers the makeover of the locations where you execute your routines, as well.

Take a look around your room right now. What do you see? What do you feel? Does your room mirror your personality?

What type of person do you strive to be? Are you an artist, a thinker, a grinder, a dreamer? How would you feel about spending your time in a room that reflects all of these things? Create the type of environment you'd feel the most comfortable and inspired in.

Do you ever get lost on Pinterest or home decoration sites, gazing at pictures of houses that are neat and nicely decorated, colorful or monochromic, modern or old fashioned rooms, and decorations? Do you feel that heart-squeezing urge to be in that place, to surround yourself with it and start creating something extraordinary in it?

If you do, it means that you have an idea what type of environment you'd love to live in. Your task is simple: slowly, but purposefully, refurbish at least your own room as the one you'd love to live in.

If you're married or live with somebody, talk about redecorating with your partner, and try to agree to some changes that you both would find appealing. If you can't get on board about bedroom refurbishment, just pick another room in the house—the kitchen, living room, guest room—it doesn't matter. Create one place in the house which will be the external epitome of your inside world.

Begin by tidying up the room. A neat environment lends itself to quality relaxation time and better sleep.

You don't have to stress about the refurbishment. If you don't have the time or money for doing it all at once, just change something, a little, as frequently as you can. Plan and design your "creativity cave" in real life too. You can do it on a piece of paper, in "Sims 4", or a proper designer program, whatever you wish. Put as many details in the design as you can. Do not leave out any decoration. Make it detailed so you can see the whole picture before your eyes.

When you are done with the planning and designing, implement the desired changes, starting with smaller items like decorations.

This is not an evening routine per se, however it is essential to feel good in your environment. You'll feel more comfortable, you'll be able to draw strength from an inspiring environment, and you'll feel less burnt out after a long day.

The famous fashion designer Vera Wang said the solution to avoiding burnout is decorating your room to aid in relaxation. "My bedroom is my sanctuary," Wang told *Fortune* Magazine in an interview. "It's like a refuge, and it's where I do a fair amount of designing—at least conceptually if not literally."

Stephen King has a rather unusual, but interesting expectation to consider his chilling environment appropriate, "The pillows are supposed to be pointed a certain way. The open side of the pillowcase is supposed to be pointed in toward the other side of the bed. I don't know why," he confessed in an interview.

Everyone is different, and everyone has a different concept of what is perfectly cozy for them. Find the best environment choice for you, and start creating it. You'll see how much more power you have in the morning, and how much easier it will be to relax in the evening if you love the place you go home to.

Exercise

To create your new "creative cave", first you have to get rid of the things that fill your room at the moment. When I did my de-cluttering project, I had a very organized and well-founded system based on which I selected the items I wouldn't keep. Read more about it in my book *Less Mess Less Stress*. In this book I will give you a short summary exercise to help you get your cozy environment for restful evening routines as soon as possible.

Here's what I did: I separated my things onto four separate sheets in a different room and organized them into categories—clothing, decorations, appliances, and other.

You know how much free space you need to create

your dream environment, so be as merciless on the selection as you need to be. If you only want to make minor changes, don't overdo the downsizing. I think it's a good idea to re-organize your stuff from time to time. It would seem like you moved in a new house. Maybe just switching your bed's position with your wardrobes would make a significant change to feel better. If not, there is no escape. You have to de-clutter.

Start by throwing out those things that are unusable. The thousand-year-old pajamas and the nice mug with the broken handle have to go. You wouldn't use them and wouldn't give them away, either. If you are sentimental, say goodbye to them. Be especially severe with your old underwear. You know what I mean. This is the easiest way to start getting rid of things—be it clothing or something else: start with the stuff that must go in the trash.

The next step, after you're done with the unusable, select the things you use most often and without which you couldn't imagine the sun rising in the east. To not fall into excess, keep yourself to the magic of the number three. Choose your top three shirts, top three trousers, bed sheets, decorations, photo frames, and so on.

When you've sorted out the unusable and the must-keeps comes the challenging part. The rest of your stuff. These are the things that are not for everyday use, but they are still wearable or usable. You may just need to lose ten pounds, or buy a new muffin-baking sheet to use them. (You burned the little devils in the old one so badly that you couldn't scratch the remains out. Oh, did I say you? I meant me.) These things are the hardest to select.

This process takes a bit longer to accomplish. Don't try to squeeze it into one night. Making yourself overly tired because of de-cluttering is not a good evening routine. Optimally, you shouldn't even do this in the evening. Do it on the weekend, on vacation, or holidays if you don't have anything special to do.

Back to the challenging part of the de-cluttering where you have to decide the fate of the things you don't use too often. Take each individual tool, and if you feel that you love it, that it would fit into your "creative cave" and you'd use it in the *next month*, keep it. If you feel attached, but not sure you'd use it in the next month, leave it with the rest of the things for now. Whenever you're done, put the *I will use these this month* items next to the *must keep* items.

Go through the remaining things again, and put those you feel attached to, and that you think you might use in the next six months, into a cardboard box and take these boxes to a storage space that is separate from your living space.

You can even hire a company to store these things. When we pay for something, we value it much more—and it also becomes a pain in the neck if we spend that money for nothing.

If, in that half-year period, you take anything out of those boxes to use them, cool. Keep that particular thing. But, for the rest of the things lying in the garage or in some storage unit—they have to go. You didn't need them, you probably lived just fine without them and *if, maybe, perhaps,* one day you'll need something from there, trust that you'll be able to buy it again. If we're talking about very expensive things like skiing equipment, store it for five years. It would be very pricey to buy the entire kit again. However, if you didn't touch the damn twenty-kilogram package for more than five years, start contemplating seriously about giving it away. If you go skiing less frequently that every five years, maybe it is a better deal to rent the skiing equipment on the spot.

The final category: those things that are not unusable, but you know you won't use in the next six months, or ever. Put them into a box and find the best place to donate them. I, for example, used Facebook to find a place to donate my things. I contacted a Hungarian goodwill group, and in half an hour I found a family who needed the clothes, a village school for my school supplies, and a homeless shelter for my kitchen equipment and bedroom things (quilts, pillows, whatnot). If your things have more financial than personal value, you can try to pass them on E-bay, Craigslist or other bargain sites. This way you'll make some money back on the unused tool.

Have a short, skill improvement session a few times in a week. This short evening routine can save you much more time during the day. It is like doing your homework before you go to class the next day. Classes in this sense are the major tasks you have to deal with on a daily.

What are your top priority tasks for the next day? Is there any exercise you could take to improve in the tasks' areas?

Maybe learning to type faster would save you some time at your job. You'd become more efficient. Or, taking an online course on communication would improve your ability to talk to your clients and be more confident of your presentation skills. You'd also be able to summarize your speech better and with more impact.

Pick an area you would like to improve. Spend no more than twenty minutes of your evening routine on improving that particular area. The results won't show up overnight, and twenty minutes can't guarantee you quick success, but a steady and constant improvement will come back to you over time through increased skills and efficiency.

This short self-improvement session doesn't necessarily have to be a course or a lesson. You can do crosswords, or play Sudoku. My personal new self-improvement habit for 2017 is consistent brain-conditioning exercises. With the help of the program *www.lumosity.com*,[*] I can fire up my brain at any point of the day. This program is developed by neuroscientists and develops different cognitive areas. You get new exercises each day in the form of entertaining games that challenge your memory, problem solving skills, speed, flexibility and other functions. Completing the three daily tasks doesn't take more than six minutes, it keeps my brain in shape and I have fun doing it. So, why not?

Power Down

Lay back and prepare for a more relaxed state. Deepen the moments of relaxation by unplugging for the night. When you're done with all your tasks that needed a bright light, slowly start dimming them. Ideally, you can try to replace your "creative cave's" regular lamps

---

[*]https://www.lumosity.com/en/

into ones that have adjustable brightness. Dimmer lights will help your body to release melatonin, the hormone that starts the sleep cycle. Candles can also be a good option, they are relaxing, and it is a romantic way to light your room before sleep. Remember: never leave candles unattended.

Ideally, you should go to bed early enough to be fully rested for the next day. The optimal amount of rest that your body needs is seven to eight hours. If you go to work at 7 a.m. and you have to wake at 6 a.m., you should go to bed no later than 11 p.m. Seven hours of sleep is the minimum that your body requires for peak performance.

You will be more alert and productive if you get the proper amount of rest. You'll also be healthier and feel better. All the evening routines I talk about in this book serve this one purpose: to have a good, restful sleep.

However, evening routines can backfire. You can become too active. A good book, a comforting yoga session can all make us lose track of time, and before we realize it, it's past midnight. To avoid this trap, you may need to set your alarm clock to remind yourself of your curfew.

In fact, you can set two alarms: one half an hour earlier than the time you actually want to go to bed and one for your bedtime. This way you can brush and flush without a rush, read some pages, do everything that needs to be done before sleeping. Set the other alarm for the actual sleeping time.

Consider setting your cell phone to night mode. You can also set night mode to turn on automatically. For example, let's use the interval of 9 p.m. to 7 a.m. This setting will help you prepare your eyes for sleep, since it will make the screen less bright. Over time, unnatural lights will damage your sight and perception of time.

If your job requires you to work late in the evening, and you can't power down so quickly, there is a good free program I'd recommend you to download. The program is called *F.lux*.[*] It is a free program available for Mac and Windows. It alters the color spectrum of your computer to match the patterns of sunlight in your time zone.

---

[*] https://justgetflux.com/

5

SLEEPING HABITS

I am a very moody person if I don't sleep enough, or *well enough*. The latter sometimes can compensate the former. If you have a more restful night's sleep, getting fewer hours of it won't matter as much. For example, if you sleep six hours under the right conditions, undisturbed and uninterrupted, you will feel more energized than if you'd slept for nine hours, tossing and turning.

What can you do to develop the best sleeping conditions? This chapter will strictly talk about sleeping habits.

Devise a Sleep Schedule and Stick to It

This advice can help mostly those who have the liberty to choose when to go to bed—so everybody who doesn't work in three shifts or have an unpredictable work schedule. Working people who have a fixed working schedule, freelancers, and wanderers can stick to the same sleeping schedule with a little self-restraint.

Why is This Important?

Because by doing it you'll be able to regulate your body's clock. A well-functioning body clock helps you fall asleep and stay asleep for the night. Set aside no more than eight hours for sleep. For healthy adults between the ages of 18 to 100, eight hours of sleep is enough.

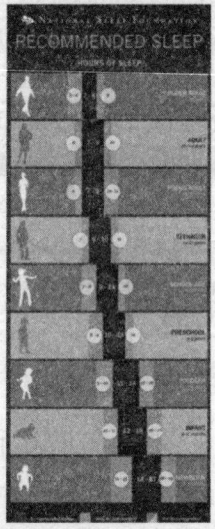

Picture I: Sleeping needs based on age

The minimum healthy amount of sleeping hours for adults is seven hours. Depending on your circadian rhythm, you might need more than eight hours of sleep to function properly, but in most cases, eight hours is the rule of thumb.

What do you have to do? Aim to go to bed and wake up at consistent times. Yes, even on the weekends. Try to stick to a one-hour difference, tops. If there is a movie on TV that would end two hours later than your regular bedtime, just record it and watch it in the morning. You might not feel tired in the evening, but you will definitely feel even a two-hour "delay" in your regular sleeping schedule the next day. Be consistent and reinforce your sleeping cycle.

Don't oversleep. If you sleep longer on the weekends, that won't help your cause. You'll just mess your body clock up and you'll experience symptoms similar to jet lag during the day. Have you ever felt like the more you slept, the more tired you felt? Then you know what I mean.

What Do You Do When You Can't Fall Asleep?

Have you ever had that annoying experience when you try to sleep with all your might, but somehow, you just can't? You know you have to wake early. The more the minutes pass by during this irritating bout of insomnia, the angrier you become. When you look at the clock and see it is 1 a.m., you get so stressed about the little amount of time you have left to sleep that you ruin your last chance for resting. At 5 a.m., you give up. You start getting ready and wait for the alarm to ring at six. When it does and you know you have to go, miraculously, the strong conviction hits you that now you could fall asleep.

There is something you can do to avoid this situation: If you can't fall asleep within twenty-something minutes after you go to the bed, don't force it. Just leave your bedroom. Go to your living room or kitchen and do something relaxing—or boring. Read a book or listen to some meditative music. When you feel tired enough, crawl back to bed and try to sleep again. Don't stay in the dark with your frustration over sleeplessness.

What about Napping?

While afternoon napping can be a good way to make up for the sleep you missed the previous night, it can backfire in the evening if you're not smart about it. Don't nap for more than twenty minutes and try doing it in the early afternoon, otherwise you won't be able to fall asleep easily at night and you'll become the insomniac monster I talked about before.

Don't Let the Post-Dinner Drowsiness Drive You to Bed

Research has proven that the best time to consume your dinner is at least two to three hours before going to sleep. This is a good rule, however, there is an enemy you'll have to fight because of early dinner/post-dinner drowsiness.

If you feel drawn to bed after dinner long before your sleeping time, resist the urge to melt away on your couch. It's better to do something that takes a mild amount of effort, like going for a walk, doing some chores, or talking to someone. I recommend an evening walk the most—as presented in the previous chapters. Walking outside will wash away even the smallest chance for you to give in to the drowsiness devil and lie on the couch.

What Do You Do if You Wake Up at Night and Can't Go Back to Sleep

Don't focus on the "oh, no, I can't fall back to sleep" panic-mongering voice in your brain. In order to stay out of your head, you need to shift focus to your body—like your breathing, for example. Practice deep-breathing exercises. Take a breath. Inhale. Exhale. Feel the air stretching your lungs.

In most cases, I start "writing" my fiction book in my head when I have trouble sleeping. I start thinking about the characters in my book and imagining what they are doing and how the narrative would progress. I set an imaginary milestone in my head for how far along I want to construct the story in that particular phase of sleeplessness. I never achieve this goal because I fall asleep before I realize it. I'm not sure if it will work for you, but for me, thinking about stories I'd love to write about is the best sleeping pill.

Whether you choose breathing or story-making, the point is to make relaxation the goal, not sleeping. Even if you won't be able to fall asleep until much later, doing something relaxing is still more helpful to your body than stressing about sleeplessness is.

Stop worrying. If you wake up at night feeling

anxious about something, don't allow your brain to spiral into a dark place. It's better to make a note in your phone about your worry and postpone it till morning, or a time when you can actually do something about it. The same goes for good ideas; make a note about them and go back to sleep with the peace of mind that they won't be forgotten.

6

PREPARATIONS FOR A GOOD NIGHT'S SLEEP

In the previous chapter, I talked about how to handle sleeping hurdles. In this chapter, I will talk about how you can prevent these hurdles from ever manifesting in the first place.

Consciously Control Your Exposure to Light

There is a naturally occurring hormone in your system called melatonin. The emission of this hormone is controlled by light exposure. Melatonin is responsible for regulating your sleep-wake cycle. Your body starts producing more melatonin around the time you ought to be going to sleep, or more precisely, when it's dark. As a consequence, you'll get sleepy. Similarly, it withdraws from your system when there's light making you more alert.

In today's modern world, things are not as simple as they were for our ancestors. Electric lights, for example, can alter your body's production of melatonin. Because of a shift in your circadian rhythm, your sleeping habits will change. This is why people can get used to working night shifts.

There are some small, free tricks you can use to help your body clock regulate itself properly. For example, you can expose yourself to sunlight after waking up—ideally in the morning. If you are a coffee-drinker like me, try having your coffee outside. Walk to a park or sit in your yard, if you have one, even if it is winter. Get dressed for the weather, and for no more than five minutes, go out and sip your black gold in the natural light.

Spending more time in natural light during the day can aid your body, in general. The more sunlight you expose your body to, the more easily it will know that it is not time to get sleepy yet. If you spend your day in a dark dungeon, on the other hand, the darkness will literally make you sleepier. Darkness activates your melatonin emissions and you'll feel drowsy and tired. As the song says, "Let the sunshine in."

During the short winter days, you can use a light

therapy box to make up for the short daylight hours. Moving your desk close to the window can also be beneficial.

When darkness falls outside, try to keep your light exposure in step with it. Avoid exposing yourself to unnatural bright lights if you wish to sleep restfully in a couple of hours. This rule applies to your electronic devices too. The blue light emitted by your television, computer, phone, or other tools can be very disturbing. Use light-altering apps to minimize the disruptive effect of these devices. One good app, as I mentioned before, is f.lux.

Although for many watching TV is a favorite evening pastime, I'd advise against it. There is nothing on television that you can't catch up on the next day, so don't fear missing out. Television programs, in most cases, stimulate your brain instead of helping it disconnect. It is better to do something non-electronic before sleeping, like reading a book.

Establish the Right Surroundings

Just like in the case of evening habits, creating the right environment for sleep is also important. The environment, in this case, is your bed.

Choose a mattress and pillows that fit your comfort needs the most. Some people prefer a harder mattress while some prefer softer, bouncier ones. Try both types and see which aid your quality of sleep the best. Keep in mind that the life expectancy for a mattress is about ten years, even when it comes to the fancy ones. Change them at least as frequently as each decade.

Have comfortable pillows. Please note that the pillows you use for decoration might not be the best fit for sleeping. Pillows designed specifically for sleeping, like memory pillows, can be the best option for a restful night's sleep. Make sure your pillow is free of allergens.

Not only bed accessories matter. Make sure the room is silent and dark before trying to sleep. Light prevents melatonin from releasing and noises are disturbing too. To darken your room, you can use thick curtains, well-sealing window blinds, or a sleep mask. Make sure to have a cotton sleep mask. Masks made of polyester can become very uncomfortable, since they will make you sweat under them. For unwanted noises you can use earplugs, or change your windows to some with extra sealing.

Keep the lights down if you get up during the night. If you need some light to move around safely, try installing a dim nightlight in the hall or bathroom or using a small flashlight. This will make it easier for you to fall back asleep.

Another important aspect of your room should be its temperature. If it is too hot or too cold, your sleep won't be relaxing. Sleeping experts advise keeping your bedroom temperature between 60 and 67 degrees. If needed, use humidifiers, heating, or cooling machines. If you use air conditioning, make sure to buy a silent one and position it as far from your bed as possible.

Keep Your Nutrition in Check

Avoid caffeine, alcohol, cigarettes, and heavy meals in the evening. Eating big or spicy meals can cause indigestion. Before going to sleep, try to eat a lighter meal instead of a full-blown steak. Sugar and carbs like pasta, bread, and white rice can cause wakefulness, so avoid eating them before sleeping.

Don't overdo drinking water, either. If you didn't drink the recommended amount of liquids during the day, don't try to make up for it before sleep. You'll be forced to make quite a few trips to the place where even the king goes alone. Drink only a little bit before going to bed, no more than 16 oz. of water—preferably an hour before sleeping.

I know that most of my tips sound obvious. If this is the case, follow them. If you're not doing the obvious, don't expect your quality of sleep to improve. Achieving a restful night's sleep doesn't require too many or too complicated actions. Just make sure to respect all the little obvious steps to get a restful sleep. If, however, respecting these steps won't help you with your sleep, I strongly recommend you to turn to a doctor or sleep specialist. For normal sleeping problems, my advice should be sufficient. For chronic issues, you need a doctor. You may want to record your sleeping patterns in a sleep diary for a few weeks so when you go to a doctor, you can show your notes and the doctor can evaluate your issues.

7

EVENING ROUTINE FOR PARENTS

"Always kiss your children goodnight, even if they're already asleep."

—H. Jackson Brown, Jr.

Five years have passed since John started changing his evening routines. Many things changed since then. He got married, and they just welcomed their first children—twins. Both of these changes made it impossible for John to go on with his regular evening habits. When he was single, it was easy to divide his time as he wanted. Now, he has to plan in a way to meet his wife's schedule and also the children's.

This doesn't mean that what I wrote earlier in the book loses its validity for parents. All those evening habits mentioned until now are manageable when living with somebody or having kids. The emphasis in John's story is on the change that appeared in his life. It would be a pity to lose the ingrained good habits just because of major life changes. In this chapter I will talk about how to adjust them to new, changed circumstances. Adjustment can be a bit uncomfortable, but it's worth trying.

Does your "home after work" experience start something like this? You walk in the door, super tired from work, all of your children fly out of their rooms to tell you what the highlight of their day was at school, dancing class and after? They are all ears and eyes when asking for dinner, one has already finished homework that needs immediate checking, and your spouse needs attention, too. And all these events take place before you even have time to change into your cozy home shoes?

Keeping up with your evening routines in this scenario is as possible as the missions of Tom Cruise in the *Mission Impossible* movie franchise. But, he always succeeded in the end, and so can you. Just be flexible and don't give up.

The first challenge is to plan a routine for your family and plan a routine for yourself. This means you sometimes have to keep up with two parallel routines at the same time.

Start with thinking about your evening essentials: what are those things you want to accomplish this evening?

In the previous chapters, I presented many options that can make your evening better, but you don't have to do all the exercises each evening. They are options. I believe that the only exercise that can't be skipped is *the planning for the next day*. All the others can be taken more smoothly.

For example, you can divide them between your weekdays: on Mondays, Wednesdays, and Saturdays you do stretching and reading, on Tuesdays and Thursdays you can do short course-sections to improve your skills in something, Fridays and Sundays you may take a relaxation bath and meditate. Remember, I said this is a sample schedule, you can organize it as you wish.

When you know what your evening routine priorities are, collect what are the specific needs of your family every night. There are some must-be–done, like dinner and cleaning up. You also need to make sure the kids have their showers, brush their teeth and pick out clothes for them for the next day. These mostly apply when your kids are younger.

Don't forget, evening routines are your plans for the evening. They are not a must. Nobody fires you if you don't follow them perfectly. Don't stress about them, make changes when you need. This is one secret of successful parenting routines.

Flexibility

Force majeure events can happen every minute with children. If you are too stiff with your plans, you might become angry, impatient and stressed. Adding that you are tired, you may say or do things that you'll regret later.

Be realistic about the expectations you set for yourself. You have limited energy. You can't meet all the needs around you without paying a price for it. This price can be insufficient sleep, over-exhaustion, stress, and impatience. If you sap your energy daily, it can turn into severe physical or mental illnesses.

Accept that there will be no day when you'll go to sleep knowing that you finished absolutely everything you had planned. That's normal. At the end of the day, the most important evening routine is to sleep. That is the number one priority. Get enough rest to be ready for the next day. The other plans are secondary. All the routines I mentioned in this book so far can be very helpful, and they indeed level up your evening and the next day. However, if you don't sleep enough they will lose a lot of their positive impact.

Exercise

I come from a post-communist country where the share of equal labor was one of our society's pillars—at least in theory. Even though it didn't work out so well on a national level, it can bring good results in a small community, like… your family.

Involve your partner and children in evening routines that serve the "common good." Old family patterns where the wife has to take care of the children and household, and the husband goes to work and brings the money home are outdated. There is no shame for a man to do chores, or even take a paternity leave. In Nordic countries in Europe, there is a growing trend for paternity leave. Anu Partanen in her book, *The Nordic Theory of Everything: In Search of a Better Life*, opens the black box of the key differences in US and Nordic family models.

If the household has dual income, isn't it only fair the same two people take care of the chores too? If your partner is not very open to helping you, open a discussion about it. Don't be aggressive or judgmental, that type of persuasion never works.

List out all the housework that needs to be done in a week. Include everything that comes to mind: tidying up the house, grocery shopping, gardening, cooking, laundry, paying bills, and all the tasks that your child (and/or your pet) needs.

When you have a clear picture about what are the key tasks you should share, plan a fun weekend with your partner. Schedule activities you know your partner likes. Yes, I know, it's borderline bribing, but the goal justifies the means. The point is to create a nice and chill atmosphere. Don't bring up this topic during a tense time, and don't be demanding or condescending with your request.

As Dale Carnegie stated in his book *How to Win Friends and Influence People*, first highlight the good qualities of a person, criticize or ask for something only after. This way people accept criticism easier and are more eager to help.

For example, tell your partner how much you appreciate the work they already do. You can highlight some specific things, in men's case taking the rubbish out or washing the car; in women's case taking care of the children's homework or the dishes. Then put your list of weekly chores in front of them, simply and plainly. Tell how much help it would be if you could get rid of the burden of this task and that task. You could become more energetic, could have some time for yourself, be less stressed and everybody would be much happier.

Be patient. Pick only a few chores that you need the most help with at first. Tell your partner that you think they could execute this particular task much better, faster than you anyway. *Give them a good reputation to live up to.*[2] This is another tiny form of manipulation, especially if it is not true that your partner can do the task better. If you find it immoral, don't add it to your convincing speech.

When your partner accepts your requests, divide the housework. Keep in mind what for you may be a routine, for your mate can be a high-level challenge. Make sure to help them out with as many details as possible to avoid future conflicts. For example, what is the detergent you use for washing the clothes? How often do the flowers need to be watered? It's your task to "domesticate" your partner to become the ultimate chore partner, too.

Do not forget to thank your mate for their efforts. Emphasize how good of a team you are. Becoming so synchronized at home can improve your relationship's quality a lot.

This process will take time, and it will seem tiring in the beginning. From experience I can tell you how frustrating it can be to watch my significant other struggling with a task for fifteen minutes when I know I could do that task in five. But I remind myself that it is a fifteen-minute struggle for him, too. He does it for my sake and he wouldn't do it for his own. So, I take a deep breath, I tell him that he is doing a great job, and then I share some tips with him how he could do it more efficiently.

Today, he is much more familiar with "his part of the chores" and I feel we make a great team. My respect toward him grew a lot, and so did his toward me. Now he understands how many things I had to do, besides working, to keep the household afloat. I feel really loved by him, knowing how many things he does to help me out.

How to Involve Your Children in Housework

If you really want to transform your family life into a little kolkhoz (a form of collective farm), involve your children in chores, too.

This can bring many beneficial results, beyond the practical, that is less work on your shoulders. For example, children who experience an appreciation of working at an early age tend to turn out to be more responsible, less spendthrift and work-shy young adults, than those who always get everything on a silver plate.

Under normal circumstances, parents love their children and they want the best for them. Doing everything for your children when they are capable of doing some tasks individually is not the best you can do for them as a parent.

If children experience what it means to work for simple things, like a clean plate or a clean bed, fresh food, or even earning money, they will learn to value it early. They will also become more respectful toward their parents. They can weigh their parents' hardships—even if only a little. Ironically, those children who are treated with spoiling love are often rude and disrespectful with their parents.

How Can You Involve Your Children in Housework?

Meanwhile, it's easy to explain to your partner why you need help simply by showing them a piece of paper with the chores listed—plus the incentive of a football match or shopping tour, it won't be the same with your kids. If you think convincing your partner to help is challenging, convincing a six, ten or twelve-year-old is ten times harder.

Kids don't like doing housework for the same reason as adults: these tasks are generally boring. It's the nature of chores. The satisfaction of getting the laundry washed is not a very big one, especially in the age of video games.

Trying to convince children to help can end up in a family battle, a lot of nagging, screaming and threatening. At the end, the kid will run away in anger or crying, you'll regret your words and will be angry at your kids' resistance at the same time. Nothing will get done.

I advise you not to use chores as punishment. If your kid misbehaves, don't give them a consequence of vacuuming, for example. The simple reason behind it is a psychological one. Like Pavlov's dog, the kid will connect chores with punishment, negative feelings or even fear. Your child will hate housework, and try to evade it. Growing up, he or she will still avoid it.

James Kimmel, a PhD in psychology from New York University, and director of For Children—A Child Therapy Center suggests, "If the chores hinder the child greatly from other more desirable activities, the child is then receiving 'double' punishment, which is not only unfair, but doubly painful. The assignment of chores as punishment can lead children to resent and hate the chores that need to be accepted as a natural part of learning, working, and caring for oneself and others."

However, there are other ways to get your kid on board with household helping. Since the biggest disadvantage of chores is that it's boring, the best way to "sell" it is to make the convincing process more interesting.

Here are some tips from the *Life as Mama*[3] website that were shared on Facebook more than 35,000 times. In my book I will share three of these tips. To see the rest of their fantastic ideas, check out the site in the link above.

Exercise

The first tip I'll share with you is one that Life as Mama calls "Work for Hire". Set up a plaque on the wall and write on it "Work for Hire". When there is a chore that your kid can do, write the task on a piece of paper and also how much "salary" you will pay for it—one dollar, two dollars. Maybe three for harder, longer or weekend "shifts".

This is a very productive and easy way to teach your kid a "valuable lesson about work ethic."

I read an article about a six-year-old who wanted to buy a bunk bed. His parents used the "work for hire" motivation system and the kid quickly realized that taking advantage of this possibility he could earn real money. After six months, he could buy his dream bed. His parents were so proud of him, and with a good reason.

The second tip is called the "Scratch off chore sheet." You know those lottery tickets where you have to scratch off the silver area to find out if it is a winning ticket? Does it keep you intrigued, excited about what the result will be? If a lottery ticket can fire adults up, imagine how fired up a child could be?

Life as Mama talks about a simple chore sheet, but I think you can boost it a bit. For each week, prepare twelve little windows. Under seven of them write a chore for your child—and now comes the magic. Under two windows write a reward, two windows that say "scratch another window", and leave one window empty. This way the excitement and motivation will be even higher. Also, it can become a great family entertainment.

The third idea is similar to rewards cards at some shops. If you eat there, you get a stamp on your fidelity card. After nine stamps, the tenth meal is free. Based on this concept, create a Chore Card. After each chore is done, your kid receives a stamp on the little card. After X-number of occasions, they get a reward.

You can get creative with these cards. The first card can be a regular ten-stamp bronze card. After completing three simple cards, they can upgrade to a fifteen or twenty-stamp silver card. With this card they get a bigger reward. They can then upgrade to golden and platinum cards. The reward for a platinum card can be something that keeps kids really motivated to fight for, like a trip to Disney Land or a play station with some games, depending on your budget.

This is a simple gamification process. You apply gaming elements and principles in a non-game context. The collecting methods can be different: point earnings, badges, leveling up, rankings, special privileges and so on. If you are familiar with any online game, they all are built upon these structures. Some of these games can cause serious addictions because of the aforementioned elements. Wouldn't it be better for your child to get hooked on chores instead of a noisy game?

If you have more than one child, it can be a good motivational approach to make a friendly competition between them. When I was a kid, my grandmother said who finished soup first would be the angel. I don't know why it was so motivating to me to become the angel, but I ate the soup as though my life depended on it, even if I didn't like it. Tricky grandma, wasn't she? It was an innocent but efficient competition spirit booster.

Using the third method I presented, the Chore Card, you can challenge your kids with the promise of an extra gift—the one who completes the Chore Card first will get the regular gift and something else. This way they will become motivated to do chores for you, not only for the extra gift, but winning over their siblings.

If you are against competition between your kids, as some parents are and I respect that, you can try to motivate them to cooperate. For example, if they do a chore together, helping each other, they get double stamps.

It really depends on you how stressful or fun your family-related evening routines will be. If you are patient and creative enough, the whole evening craziness can turn into a big family cooperation to get everything done.

The tips on how to motivate your kids to do chores could be applied to adults, too. If you don't have children yet, the Chore Card, for example, can be turned into a fun, kinky game. I really leave this one to your imagination.

I'll share with you a method that my parents used when I was smaller. They had a big circle of friends, all having children. Each week someone organized a child's day, mostly on Friday, and all of us kids had a sleepover at that place. This way the other families could enjoy a "childless" evening and could catch up with chores, or do other things. Each week another family hosted the event, so usually everybody had one day a month when they had to put up with four-five unruly little monsters. But, in exchange they had three days a month when they could have an evening to themselves.

Some of the world's busiest people opened up about how they manage their evening routines with their children in different interviews.

Sheryl Sandberg, the Chief Operating Officer of Facebook and author of the bestselling book *Lean In*, gets out of the office at the same time every evening. She confessed that she wouldn't mind staying at the office longer, but it is very important for her to have dinner with her children. "I walk out of this office every day at 5:30 p.m. so [that] I'm home for dinner with my kids at 6 p.m.," she told *INC*.[4] To be able to comply with her goal of family time, she often stays up late to finish answering emails and other tasks she had left in the office. However, when she is ready to sleep she turns off all her electronic devices to enjoy an uninterrupted night.

Barack Obama, former president of the United States, also finds it very important to spend his evening with his family. "Have dinner with the family, hang out with the kids, and put them to bed about 8:30 p.m. And then, I'll probably read briefing papers or do paperwork or write stuff until about 11:30 p.m., and then I usually have about a half hour to read before I go to bed... about midnight, 12:30 a.m.—sometimes a little later," he said in an interview with Newsweek.

John and his wife took a short vacation. They left the kids at the grandparents' so they could have undisturbed quality time to talk about how to reorganize their days. Both of them had some evening habits, which they could manage to do before their children arrived, but recently their evenings ended up in chaos.

Both of them listed their most important evening routines that they wouldn't like to neglect in the future. When they had completed their lists, they compared them and agreed upon a division of labor that would allow them to practice their beloved routines.

It was a fruitful vacation, and its positive effects shortly followed. Now that they knew what the other's needs were, they could synchronize their actions. They both did chores, spent some time with their children, and had free time to do their routines. It was just a matter of communication and coordination.

8

WHAT ABOUT THOSE WHO CAN'T SLEEP EARLY?

This book discussed the hurdles and solutions for those who have to get up early. However, there are many professions and professionals who can't, don't have to or don't want to sleep and get up early.

Some people work night shifts, others have their own businesses and their most creative hours are the ones in the evening. Some folks are "night owls" and so on. Although most healthy living specialists, and high achievers consider the early sleep—wake up combo as the key to success, there are some people who couldn't live by those standards.

This chapter helps them to establish better sleeping habits. I avoid the term evening habit on purpose because the habit they practice is not in the evening.

Studies showed that about twenty percent of people are night owls.[5] In some cases, this attributive is coded in our genetics. Some people have their circadian rhythm in a different time zone than the "normal people." The opposite is also true. About twenty percent of the population is an early bird, with the circadian rhythm twisted to the other edge. They wake up notoriously early.

But What is a Night Owl More Precisely?

They are those people who can't sleep early. They go to bed late in the nighttime and tend to wake up late in the forenoon. In our adolescence, many of us experience a temporary night owl-ness because of our hormonal changes. Most people outgrow this temporary condition as soon as the hormonal changes stabilize. A fifth of the population, however, never changes. They stay night owls.

Waking up early can be a real problem for genetically coded night owls. They can't really help their nature, thus their job becomes a burden, they don't perform as well in the morning, and even if they force themselves to go to bed early, their sleep won't be as good as those with normal circadian rhythm.

Night owls need different habits to be well-rested, healthy, and happy. Good sleep is completely achievable if you are not an early bird, don't worry. I collected the best tips sleeping specialists recommend for those who like to stay up late in the night.

It doesn't matter when but make sure you are getting enough sleeping hours. The key issue for night owls is that they wouldn't sleep early but they must wake early. Sometimes they get not more than four, five hours' sleep, which on long term, can have serious consequences. It doesn't matter how long you sleep in the weekends, you can't make up for the hours lost during the week. Weekday sleep deprivation leads to physical and mental health problems.

Some people are well-off with six hours of sleep, but if you are not one of them, you have to think about how you can manage to jam more sleeping hours in your schedule. Sleeping earlier is always an option. It is going to be hard in the beginning but with practice, an eye mask and earplugs, you can eventually train yourself to sleep early. Even one, one and a half hours in plus can make a huge difference.

If you can't or don't want to change your evening (night) routines, there's no other way around, you have to change your morning routines. If you study, choose afternoon classes rather than morning ones. If you work, try to switch to a flexible schedule or change careers where you can work later in the day. It seems a harsh change but on the long run, your health is more important than any job in the world.

A third—and worst, but better than nothing—option is having short naps, or a longer nap in the afternoon. Afternoon naps, however, never give you the same amount of sleeping benefits as a nighttime sleep. Also, having a nap in the afternoon dooms you to go to bed later in the evening since you won't feel tired early enough. Choose this option only if there is no chance you can change something about the former two options above.

Try to keep yourself to schedules. While early birds work as a clock, they go to bed almost always at the same time, night owls' sleeping schedule can fluctuate. One day at 2 a.m., the other day at 4 a.m. Irregular sleeping habits are very harmful since your body will never be able to adjust to a fixed amount of sleep. Less sleep will make you powerless and moody the next day.

Having a predictable, fixed sleeping schedule is much more important for night owls since they often get less sleep as people with normal circadian rhythm. Try to keep yourself to your fixed sleeping schedule in the weekend, as well.

Night owls' brain is more active in the evening. This is one reason why they don't feel sleepy late in the night. To be able to sleep earlier, you have to try to shut your mind. Powering down earlier, using F.lux on your computer starting from 6 p.m., meditating, and reading something rather boring can all help to tire your brain. You have to do these practices early enough to exhaust your mind well enough by the desired sleep time.

Avoid distractions in the bedroom. No TV, tablet, computer, or phone is allowed. You just peek onto social media and you get lost on the internet shopping and realize five hours later that five hours have passed. Nope, no electronics for you. Keep your room dark but cozy. Have some candles around which have dim lights. If you notice anything that distracts you from sleep, get rid of it. If your pillow is uncomfortable, get rid of it.

Don't binge. Night owls are more likely to gain extra pounds because of nighttime binging. They stay up late, so they have more opportunity to munch this and that. Also, they often don't sleep more than five–six hours. This means they can eat in a straight eighteen–nineteen hour circle.

Be aware about your eating opportunities and say no to snacks on purpose. Eating something heavy not only hurts your shape, but also causes indigestion, which is one of the greatest enemies of a restful sleep. If you must munch something, choose some healthy vegetables like carrots, celery, or nuts like unsalted almonds or walnuts.

Remember, alcohol, nicotine and caffeine are not aiding your sleep. Quite the contrary, they disturb the restful sleeping. Although not drinking caffeine after 3 p.m–4 p.m. p.m. is kind of obvious, the other two are not so much. Just like caffeine, nicotine is a drug and a stimulant, and affects your sleeping substantially—especially if you smoke before going to bed.

Better quit smoking, but if you must, have your last one three-four hours before sleeping. Researchers at the University of Rochester Medical Center found that smoking, namely its active ingredient, nicotine, can alter your natural circadian rhythm, causing shallow sleep and sleeping disruptions. Smokers sleep more restless and snore more often than non-smokers. A study of University of Florida in 2013 proved that smokers lose 1.2 minutes of sleep for every cigarette they had during the day.

According to Sleep Foundation, alcohol may help you fall asleep quicker it will also "help" waking up more often in the night. Alcohol "may affect the normal production of chemicals in the body that trigger sleepiness when you've been awake for a long time, and subside once you've had enough sleep. After drinking, production of adenosine (a sleep-inducing chemical in the brain) is increased, allowing for a fast onset of sleep. But it subsides as quickly as it came, making you more likely to wake up before you're truly rested."[6]

Alcohol consumption before sleeping also blocks REM sleep. This type of sleep is considered to be the most restorative type of sleep. Less REM sleep means less focus, more anger and impatience the next day.

Forget about pumping iron in the evening. While many people feel their strength peaks in the evening, heavy cardio or weight workout fires up your metabolism, making your body too energized to sleep. Don't work out heavy after 8 p.m. if you wish to sleep around 11 p.m. Do yoga, or regular stretching instead.

Remember, enough sleep helps you look fit and healthy. Lack of sleep turns your face long, tired and less attractive.

The tips I collected apply for those night owls who can't have enough sleep because of work, school or other obligations. If you are a night owl, and can have your eight hours sleep, please, go work out at midnight if you please. In that case reschedule my tips to your numbers. The main logic of my tips still apply. Don't eat, drink, smoke, workout a few hours before sleeping. If that sleeping happens at 3 a.m., calculate the hours accordingly.

9

DO'S AND DON'TS

"The best way to make your dreams come true is to wake up."

—Paul Valéry

I am a strong believer of the saying, "Repetition is the mother of knowledge." In this chapter, I'll recap what are the best things you can do in your evening and what are the worst. This book is a collection of many of the best practices you can do in the evening. This doesn't mean that you should do them all each evening—or ever. If you implement just one or two techniques in your evening routine, that is already a huge step forward.

I presented you some options and it's up to you

which ones you choose to use. You can change them to fit more to your schedule. You can add or take away some aspects of the exercises so they serve your needs in the best way possible.

You can also schedule a different exercise for each evening. This way you can try them all and discover which ones you need the most. You do evening routines for yourself, for your own good. They shouldn't cause you any stress. They are supposed to serve the opposite purpose. Stay flexible, don't consider these routines as a must but as tools to better your life.

Evening Do's:

1. Complement your morning routines with solid evening routines. They will help you improve your focus, memory and creativity throughout the day.
2. Process your day in the evening.
3. Ask yourself the following questions regarding the highlights of your day:

    What did I do regarding the task that went well?
    What did I do regarding the task that didn't go well?
    What did I not do regarding the task that made it not go so well?

What did I not do regarding the task that made it go well?

How can I improve?

4. Processing your day will often help you to remember tasks that you did not accomplish. Write them down, and put them in a visible place.
5. Plan your next day. Write down step-by-step instructions for everything you want to do the next day. When you're finished, order your daily tasks based on importance. Which ones have top priority? Which are not so urgent? The top items are the tasks you want to spend your time on.
6. Learn to say no. You don't have to be rude about it, but draw a clear line. Where others' needs deter you from yours, say no.
7. Avoid procrastination.
8. Decrease decision fatigue: The fewer decisions you have to make, the less tired you'll be at the end of the day—both physically and mentally. You'll have more energy and capacity to do things for yourself in the evening. Prepare your breakfast in advance and maybe lunch for work, too. Decide and prepare what you will wear the next day. Eventually you can plan your week in advance.

9. Take a short walk after dinner.
10. Have an early dinner. The reason for an early dinner is the promise of a more restful sleep.
11. A place for everything and everything in its place: put unused items away before you sleep.
12. Relax. Take a bath, light candles, listen to meditation music—let go of the stress of the day.
13. If you are flexible, or just genuinely interested, do a short and relaxing yoga session.
14. Try back-stretching exercises. It can be especially beneficial if you work in an office.
15. Read before sleeping. Keep some books on your nightstand. Have multiple genres so you can pick the one that fits your mood the best each day.
16. Practice gratitude. Regardless of what happened that day, say thank you, and be grateful that you got to live through this day.
17. Hydrate. Don't forget that your body won't get any hydration for seven or eight hours when you sleep. Keep a bottle of water next to your bed and drink a glass before sleeping.
18. Create the right environment. A place where you hate, dislike, or feel neutral to be is demotivating. De-clutter your creativity cave by selecting your things based on the following categories: must keeps, unusable,

use it in one month, use it within six months, and giveaways.

19. For your personal development session, pick an area you would like to improve. Spend no more than twenty minutes of your evening routine on improving that particular area.

20. Power down. Turn off your computer and your TV. Switch the bright lights to less bright ones. Ideally, try to replace your "creative cave's" regular lamps into ones that have adjustable brightness.

21. Plan a routine for your family and plan a routine for yourself.

22. Divide routines between your days. For example you can divide them between your weekdays: on Mondays, Wednesdays and Saturdays you may do stretching and reading, on Tuesdays and Thursdays you do short course-sections to improve your skills in something, Fridays and Sundays you take a relaxation bath and meditate.

23. Be realistic about the expectations you set for yourself regarding the amount of routines you may jam into your evening. You have limited energy. Accept that there might be no single day ever when you'll go to sleep knowing that you finished absolutely everything you planned.

24. List out all the housework that needs to be done in a week. When you have a transparent and clear picture about what the key tasks you should share doing are, plan a fun weekend plan with your partner.
25. Trying to convince children to help can end up in a family battle. Don't use chores as punishment. The biggest disadvantage of chores is that it's boring, the best way to "sell" it is to make the process more interesting.
26. Each week, a couple in your circle could organize a children play day, usually on a Friday, and all the kids can have a sleepover at that place. This way the other families could enjoy a "childless" evening.

Evening Don'ts:

1. Don't stay up late if you have to wake up early in the morning. At least, don't do it on long term, otherwise your daily energy level and concentration will significantly decrease.
2. Don't live your life on social media.
3. Don't rationalize your bad habits, like staying up late or wasting a lot of time with valueless activities.
4. Don't have a late dinner.
5. Don't ignore your needs as a human. Stop being dedicated to everything and everyone but yourself.

6. Without targets, days can turn into a pointless mass of hours.
7. Don't give in to distractions. Take control of the things you can influence. Cut your social media time and make coffee breaks shorter, and like magic, you'll win precious hours in your life. Be strong and resist temptations.
8. Don't rush with your evening routines. There is no point doing them if you stress about them. Select only as many routines for a day as you are able to finish properly, without becoming anxious.
9. Don't stick to your guns. If you planned your evening in a certain way, but something intervenes, be flexible and postpone your routine tasks for later.
10. Don't expect changing your evening habits to be easy. Adopting a stable and well-structured evening routine takes time and dedication. It means you have to change your entire life-style. Start slowly, and only when you feel comfortable with your newly adopted habits, introduce a new one.
11. Don't skip the planning part. If you take only one piece of advice from this book, let that be the planning of your next day.
12. Don't forget that you have limited energy. You might not feel it yet, but all the sleepless nights, stressful

days and unfulfilled wishes gather and backfire when you least expect it. Your health is the greatest gift. Don't handle it recklessly. Remember the words of the Dalai Lama: "Man surprises me most about humanity. Because he sacrifices his health to make money. Then he sacrifices money to recuperate his health."

I wish you all the best with your new evening routines. I hope you could gather some gems among my words that you'll successfully implement in your evening routine.

"In the end, winning is sleeping better."

—Jodie Foster

Sleep well, and start your day with a healthy, wholehearted, energetic smile on your face.

I believe in you!

Zoe

REFERENCE

Carnegie, Dale. *"How to Win Friends and Influence People."* Simon & Schuster, Reissue Edition. ISBN: 1439167346. 2009.

Geddes, Linda. *"First Physical Evidence of Why You're an Owl or a Lark."* New Scientist. 2013. https://www.newscientist.com/article/dn24292-first-physical-evidence-of-why-youre-an-owl-or-a-lark/#.VHzEkNbTxsP.

Life As Mama. *"10 Brilliant Ideas To Motivate Your Children To Do Chores."* Life As Mama. http://lifeasmama.com/10-brilliant-ideas-to-motivate-your-children-to-do-chores/10/ .

National Sleep Foundation. *"How Alcohol Affects the Quality—and Quantity—of Sleep."* National Sleep Foundation. https://sleepfoundation.org/sleep-topics/how-alcohol-affects-sleep.

Picture I. National Sleep Foundation. *"Healthy Sleep Tips."* National Sleep Foundation. https://sleepfoundation.org/sleep-tools-tips/healthy-sleep-tips.

Stillman, Jessica. "*Sheryl Sandberg Leaves Work at 5:30. Why Can't You?*" Inc. 2012. https://www.inc.com/jessica-stillman/facebook-sheryl-sandberg-can-leave-early-why-arent-you.html.

COMMUNICATION AND CONFIDENCE COACHING

By working with me you can expect to gain a better understanding of yourself, and the hope you need to change your life for the better. I will help you understand everybody around you better starting with yourself. My three main goals are to help you:

- Embrace discomfort to break down your negative beliefs.
- Find your strengths and focus on them.
- Bring out the side of you that is totally comfortable with yourself and your environment.

I have a unique approach to coaching. The entire lesson is composed of two parts:

Interpersonal Skills Development

Do your palms sweat and your heart pound when you enter in a room full of strangers? Do you feel awkward when somebody starts a conversation with you? Do you fear you'll run out of things to say and wish you could just talk casually with everybody?

Then this course was made for you!

In this section, I'll help you learn how to communicate with others, how to be presentable, and how to always make a great impression. Humans are social beings and since you live among them you can never underestimate the importance of social skills. If you have them you can be one hundred percent present and aware in any situation. I have been studying and developing communication and real-life social interaction skills for more than ten years. I've written ten books—all of them Amazon bestsellers—on the topic. I can help you, please let me!

Here you will learn:

- How to start conversations and keep them going with anybody.
- How to "win friends and influence people".
- Airy, pleasant ways to be more charming and likable.

- How to be the life of the party.
- Tips on how to handle difficult conversations and people.

I'll teach you how to be the person everyone notices when you enter the room, the person who instantly sparks people's interest and can talk easily to anyone.

Intrapersonal Skills Development

Is the mirror your worst enemy? Or the scale? Or both? Do you feel uncomfortable with who you are? Do you sometimes feel your days are passing by without any purpose? Is sleeping your favorite activity? Do you wish you were somewhere else, maybe someone else?

If any of these statements apply to you then you have work to do. Living with self-contempt, regrets, and frustration is not sustainable. In this part of the coaching I will help you to accept and recover from any inner struggles you have. With honesty and commitment, I will guide you to let go of old wounds, and help you find your strengths and develop them in order to bring out the best in yourself.

I'll help you:

- to discover the root cause of your problems;

- recover from childhood traumas;
- communicate with yourself objectively and silence the malicious voices in your head;
- build confidence and self-respect, and learn to be persistent and get what you want.

If you're interested, apply here: http://www.zoemckey.com/contact/.

ENDNOTES

1. Picture I. National Sleep Foundation. *"Healthy Sleep Tips."* National Sleep Foundation. https://sleepfoundation.org/sleep-tools-tips/healthy-sleep-tips
2. Carnegie, Dale. *"How to Win Friends and Influence People.* Simon & Schuster, Reissue Edition. ISBN: 1439167346. 2009.
3. Life As Mama. *"10 Brilliant Ideas To Motivate Your Children To Do Chores."* Life As Mama. http://lifeasmama.com/10-brilliant-ideas-to-motivate-your-children-to-do-chores/10/.
4. Stillman, Jessica. *"Sheryl Sandberg Leaves Work at 5:30. Why Can't You?"* Inc. 2012. https://www.inc.com/jessica-stillman/facebook-shcryl-sandberg-can-leave-early-why-arent-you.html.
5. Geddes, Linda. *"First Physical Evidence of Why You're an Owl or a Lark."* New Scientist. 2013. https://www.newscientist.com/article/dn24292-first-

physical-evidence-of-why-youre-an-owl-or-a-lark/#.VHzEkNbTxsP.

6   National Sleep Foundation. "*How Alcohol Affects the Quality—and Quantity—of Sleep.*" National Sleep Foundation. https://sleepfoundation.org/sleep-topics/how-alcohol-affects-sleep.